Reparations!

Earl Ofari Hutchinson

Middle Passage Press
Los Angeles, CA

Publisher's Cataloging-in-Publication Data

Names: Hutchinson, Earl Ofari.
Title: Reparations! / Earl Ofari Hutchinson.
Description: Los Angeles, CA : Middle Passage Press, 2023. | Includes
  bibliographic references and index. | Summary: Examines the many facets of
  the U.S. debate over reparations for slavery, including the history of reparations
  proposals and comparisons to payments made to other groups for injustices.
  Assesses the arguments for and against reparations and why it has become
  such a racially polarizing issue.
Identifiers: LCCN 2023908744 | ISBN 9798890749451 (pbk.)
Subjects: LCSH: African Americans -- Reparations. | Reparations for historical
  injustices -- United States. | Slavery -- United States -- Public opinion. | Racism
  -- Political aspects -- United States. | Compensation (Law) -- United States.
  | BISAC: SOCIAL SCIENCE / Discrimination. | SOCIAL SCIENCE / Slavery. |
  POLITICAL SCIENCE / Civil Rights.
Classification: LCC E185.89.R45 H88 2023 | DDC 323.1196 H--dc22
LC record available at https://lccn.loc.gov/2023908744

Table of Contents

Introduction

"....black people worked long, hard, killing days, years, centuries—and they were never paid. The value of their labor went into others' pockets—plantation owners, northern entrepreneurs, state treasuries, the United States government.

Where was the money?

Where is the money? There is a debt here."

—Randall Robinson, *The Debt: What America Owes to Blacks*

On November 20, 1989, Michigan Democratic Congressman John Conyers made history of a sort. He became the first government official to formally propose that Congress study what, whether, and how some form of reparations for slavery should be made to African Americans. The bill was sent to the House Judiciary Committee.

The Conyers call ignited the bitter debate that's raged over reparations for three decades. The bill also set the stage for much myth, controversy, misunderstanding, missteps, and division about slavery reparations that has characterized much of that debate.

Conyers did not call for Congress to make reparations payments to African Americans. He did not specify what, how, or what form any reparations should be made or taken. He did not set a timetable for payments if there were any to be made. He called solely for Congress to set up a commission to study the question. His call was for the commission "to make recommendations to the Congress on appropriate remedies and for other purposes." The commission would simply be called the "Commission to Study Reparation Proposals for African Americans."

The operative word in the proposed bill was "study." In the decades since Conyers made his landmark call, that has not changed. "Study"—not payment—remains the operative word. For most of the years after Conyers introduced the bill, Congress did nothing. Year in and year out, like clockwork, he reintroduced the bill. He was determined to keep the issue alive.

Meanwhile, others filled in the blanks and put their spin on what reparations should look like. That further fueled debate. It also firmly hardened the lines between those who back reparations and those who oppose them. It also tightened the racial divide on reparations. The overwhelming majority of Blacks in numerous polls on the issue back reparations. A solid majority of whites oppose them.

In *Reparations!* political analyst Earl Ofari Hutchinson examines the many facets of the raging debate over reparations. He explores the history of reparations proposals. He compares reparations paid to other groups for injustices, including Germany's reparations payout to Holocaust survivors, to the demand for slavery reparations. He assesses the arguments for and against reparations and why it has become such a racially polarizing issue. He asks, "Can you put a price tag on slavery reparations, and what is that price to be paid for slavery's two-century horror?" A huge part of the calamitous legacy of slavery is continuing towering economic and racial inequities. Hutchinson says that, whether one backs or opposes reparations, it's an issue that will continue to ignite prickly passions within and without America's racial fault lines.

1

The Case for Reparations

"**I**'m not giving up," Michigan Democratic congressman John Conyers boldly and confidently told a group of civil rights leaders, activists, and scholars, along with a mix of community residents on February 16, 2017. Conyers had called them to a confab at his Washington D.C. office to again challenge Congress and the nation to confront the issue of reparations for slavery.

He called the meeting twenty-eight years after he had first introduced his reparations study commission proposal in Congress. Conyers' defiant proclamation that he would never throw in the towel on the issue was as much a clarion call for action as yet another challenge to Congress to take his bill for a reparations commission out of the mothballs it had lain in for nearly three decades.

Conyers was, if anything, a hard-nosed political realist. He knew that there was zero chance that then-President Trump and the GOP-controlled Congress would lend even a limp hand to his call. But the intrepid congressman still delivered the same message that he had delivered every year since 1989 when he first introduced his bill: "Slavery is a blemish on this nation's history, and until it is formally addressed, our country's story will remain marked by this blight."

*****

It wasn't just Trump and a GOP-controlled Congress that strapped on tight blinders to the issue. They had plenty of support. Millions of Americans like them, in fact, said "no" to reparations. Polls consistently show that an overwhelming majority of whites oppose reparations to Blacks for slavery and the near-century of Jim Crow racial suffering afterward. The same polls show that a majority of Blacks back reparations.

Whether opposing or supporting reparations, the fierce debate over them was torrid. During the presidential contest in 2020, some leading Democratic presidential contenders paid some lip service to it, but they gave no sign that they were willing to make it an integral campaign issue.

Conyers knew well that the issue wouldn't go away. There were several good reasons why.

1. The U.S. government, not long dead Southern planters, bears the blame for slavery—it encoded it in Article 1 of the Constitution. This designated a Black slave as three-fifths of a person for tax and political representation purposes. It protected and nourished slavery in Article 4 by mandating that all escaped slaves found anywhere in the nation be returned to their masters. In the Dred Scott decision in 1857, the U.S. Supreme Court reaffirmed that slaves remained slaves no matter where they were taken in the United States.

2. Major institutions profited from slavery. Banks, shipping companies, and investment houses made enormous profits from financing slave purchases, investments in Southern land and products, and the transport and sale of slaves. Insurance companies made big profits from insuring slaves as property.

3. Slavery ended in 1865, but the legacy of slavery has never died. Countless reports and studies have found that in every decade since the passage of the 1964 Civil Rights Bill which formally ended legal segregation, Blacks have remained the major economic and social victims of racial discrimination. They were far more likely to live in underserved segregated neighborhoods, be refused business and housing loans, be denied promotions in corporations, and attend cash-starved, failing public schools than whites.

4. There was a direct cost to slavery's legacy. Former Federal Reserve Board Chairman Andrew Brimmer, in an opinion column in November 1993, estimated that discrimination costs Blacks ten billion dollars annually through the Black-white wage gap, denial of capital access, inadequate public services, and reduced social security and other government benefits. This was called the "black tax." The racial gap remained firm each decade since Brimmer made his challenging estimate.

5. The U.S. government had shelled out billions since the 1960s to pay for resettlement, job training, education, and health programs for refugees fleeing Communist repression. There was no national outcry when the U.S. government made special indemnity payments and provided land and social service benefits to Japanese Americans interned during World War II, or to Native Americans for the theft of lands and mineral rights, or to Philippine veterans who fought with the American army during World War II.

   Politicians and most of the public enthusiastically backed these payments as the moral and legally right thing to do.

*****

6. The reparations issue would not necessarily fuel more hatred of Blacks. Most Americans admit that slavery was a monstrous system that wreaked severe pain and suffering on America. Many major city councils by 2023 had passed resolutions, or proposed or established commissions to study reparations.

7. No legislation has been proposed, let alone passed, that mandates taxpayers pay billions to Blacks. The reparations study commission that Conyers proposed had a relatively scant price tag of fewer than ten million dollars.

8. There is a precedent for paying Blacks for past legal and moral wrongs. In 1997, then President Clinton apologized, and the U.S. government paid ten million dollars to the Black survivors and family members victimized by the syphilis experiment conducted in the 1930s by the U.S. Public Health Service. In 1994, the Florida legislature agreed to make payments to the survivors and relatives of those who lost their lives and property when a white mob destroyed the all-Black town of Rosewood in 1923. The carnage there was tacitly condoned by public officials and law enforcement officers. In 2001, the Oklahoma state legislature commission recommended payments to the survivors and their descendants of the destruction of Black neighborhoods in Tulsa by white mobs in 1921. Two plus decades later, not a penny had been paid to the handful of survivors or their families.

9. Mega-rich Blacks such as Oprah Winfrey, professional athletes such as Lebron James, or Black multi-millionaire CEOs would not receive a penny in reparations.

Most reparation advocates agree that any tax money to redress Black suffering should go into a fund to bolster funding for AIDS/HIV education and prevention, underfinanced inner-city public schools, programs to expand job skills and training, drug and alcohol counseling and rehabilitation, computer access and literacy training programs, and to improve public services for the estimated one in four Blacks still trapped in poverty.

10. In the early days of his White House tenure, former President Obama was frosty toward reparations. In the waning days of his tenure, he had second thoughts. He then said that society had a "moral obligation" to close the racial gap and that there should be a massive investment in programs to do just that. He didn't exactly call it reparations. But he came close.

It was a gingerly and polite way of putting it. But Obama did recognize that America owed a debt to Black America for past and present sins. It still does. Conyers' vow not to give up would always remain the standard cry for America to finally confront the grotesque stain of slavery and its hideous legacy. Despite the compelling case that could be made for that, the dangling question was, "Would it ever?"

2

The Case Against Reparations

He called the notion of reparations for slavery "unusual" and "interesting." He quickly added, though, in case anyone mistook this for sympathy for the reparations call that he didn't "see it happening." The speaker was then President Donald Trump. In June 2019 when he spoke about it, the reparations issue had become such a hot-button topic that Trump felt even he had to say something about it in an interview. He wasn't the only top Republican to weigh in on the issue.

Then Senate Majority Leader Mitch McConnell was even blunter. Said McConnell, it wasn't "a good idea." He dredged up the by-then set-in-stone prime reason immediately shouted by reparations opponents. That was that it made no sense to shell out billions in taxpayer dollars for something such as slavery, that had ended in 1865. Or as McConnell put it, "something that happened 150 years ago."

He didn't stop there. He claimed that the Civil War, lots of civil rights laws, and even the election of President Obama were more than ample proof that the nation had more than paid its debt. For McConnell, this was a *mea culpa* and atonement enough for slavery.

*****

It was no accident that Trump was asked about reparations that month. Following Conyers' death in 2019, Texas Democratic congresswoman Sheila Jackson vowed to take up his reparations bill in Congress. She did,

9

reintroducing it in 2021. This time there was some movement on it. Several days before Trump gave his take on the bill, the House Judiciary Subcommittee on the Constitution, Civil Rights, and Civil Liberties held a hearing on it.

Jackson was hardly the only congressperson to jump in on the issue. New Jersey Democratic Senator Cory Booker introduced an almost identical bill in the Senate. Booker took almost the exact page from Conyers' decades-long playbook: "We as a nation have not yet truly acknowledged and grappled with racism and white supremacy that has tainted this country's founding and continues to persist in those deep racial disparities and inequalities today."

Trump and McConnell gave strong hints as to just what the fate of a reparations study outcome would be if they had their say. A cursory look at the sponsors of Booker's bill confirmed that. Not one GOP senator signed on as a co-sponsor. All fourteen co-sponsors were Democrats. It was the same with Jackson's bill. Not one GOP House representative signed on to it. It wasn't just Republicans, though, who were wary of the bill and the issue.

In June 2019, Democratic presidential contender Joe Biden cast a jittery gaze over his shoulder at white conservative Democrats and independents in the crucial swing states. He did not dare risk alienating them and a quick jump onto the reparation's bandwagon might do that. Biden almost out-Trumped Trump and out McConnelled McConnell in throwing ice water on reparations. Biden told the *Washington Post*, "I'll be damned if I feel responsible to pay for what happened 300 years ago."

But two years later, in February 2021, now safely ensconced in the White House, Biden cautiously changed his tune and said he'd back the Democrats' congressional reparations study proposal. But even here he hedged his bet. He quickly noted that a study was one thing, and signing an actual bill to pay reparations was an entirely different matter. Biden could still read the poll numbers. A scant fifteen percent of whites favored reparations payment. Overall, less than thirty percent of Americans favored payments. He said no more about it.

✱✱✱✱✱

There was no guesswork about why Biden was silent. In the decades since Conyers' introduced his bill in 1989, the many polls taken on the pros and cons of reparations payments for slavery show one constant. The overwhelming majority of whites oppose slavery payments. The opponents have not just been the usual suspects. That is, the GOP, hard-core conservatives, unreconstructed bigots, right-wing echo chamber bloggers and websites, and conservative think tanks. The opposition among whites has cut across all demographic lines. That includes a lot of Democrats and even those who consider themselves moderates and liberals.

One outspoken reparations advocate assumed that the stout opposition was based on a fierce resistance to ladling out public monies to Blacks for slavery. He was wrong. He probed further and concluded, "A plurality of Americans don't believe the descendants of slaves deserve reparations."

The other two stock reasons repeatedly voiced are based on the grossly erroneous belief that Blacks have attained something approaching social and economic parity with whites. Therefore, reparations payments would be unnecessary and wasteful. Yale social psychologist Michael Kraus, who studied anti-reparation attitudes, noted, "A majority of our sample tends to think that we've made steady progress towards greater equality in wealth between families, so between black and white families. That is inconsistent with reality."

McConnell and Biden, in expressing their wariness about reparations, cited another frequently heard reason to oppose reparations. Slavery formally ended in 1865. There are no slaves still alive today. Moreover, thousands of the forbearers of whites came to this country long after slavery ended. Thus, they bear no liability for it. This latter point is also voiced by many Latino and Asian Americans who are immigrants or descendants of immigrants. They also counter that they, too, have felt the sting of racism. A majority of them oppose reparations.

One opponent summed this sentiment up: "The generation that would be paying for it has nothing to do with what was done in the past. And then you're paying people that have nothing to do with it in the past." He added, "We're all immigrants at some point, whether it was voluntary or forced."

The standard answers to the question of why there should not be payments for slavery did not form in a vacuum, nor are they driven solely by racial bigotry or ignorance— though much of that is there in abundance on the issue. The opposition has been undergirded by a seemingly solid and reasoned intellectual and political viewpoint.

This oppositional view has been honed, refined, and sharpened over time by conservative think tanks and analysts. Their arguments on the surface appear both factual and persuasive, and they make perfectly good sense to many. But it's certainly true the U.S. government and the Constitution, bolstered by an avalanche of laws on the books for centuries, have encoded segregation, inequality, and the gross exploitation of Blacks.

But the case is also made that the same government also radically revised the Constitution with the passage of the 13th, 14th, and 15th Amendments. It passed the Civil Rights Act and Voting Rights Act, as well as successive amendments and revisions that have strengthened civil rights since the 1950s.

This progress was further enhanced by legions of court rulings and decisions strengthening civil rights protections; banning job, housing, and lending discrimination; and promoting pay equity and affirmative action programs. These measures are repeatedly posed as transformative legal and institutional measures designed to redress the decades of Jim Crow racial disparities.

Opponents also insist that it's a myth that all non-Blacks have benefited from Black exclusion and racial disparities. Poor whites, immigrants, and other non-whites also have been subject to economic exclusion, social and racial disparities, and impoverishment for decades with no government helping hand to alleviate their plight.

*****

Reparations advocates continually cite reparations paid to two other groups. One is payments made by the U.S. government to Japanese Americans for their four-year illegal, unconstitutional, shameful, and disgraceful incarceration in concentration camps during World War II. They were stripped of their jobs, homes, businesses, and farms. The other is the billions the German government shelled out to Israel and to Jewish Holocaust survivors for the Nazi slaughter of millions of Jews.

The payments in both cases were made to specific individuals impacted, Japanese Americans and Jews, and their families who were still living. In the case of Germany, payments were also made directly to a nation, Israel. The money was laser-targeted, and fully accounted for.

This raises the even greater point of contention for reparations opponents: just who should get reparations. This issue even divides some passionate reparations advocates. Some argue that cash payments should be made directly to individuals. Others say the payments should go for scholarships, and to boost business and education, jobs, and housing programs. Then there are the debates over how much is owed for slave labor, what criteria would be used once a firm dollar figure is put on it, and the mechanics of how the money should be paid out.

The question of who should be the recipient of a payment in cash or kind is the ultimate break point for reparations opponents. They continually return to this question. One conservative opponent calls it a dual nightmare. It would open the door to endless legal squabbles, litigation, lawsuits, and charges of discrimination by thousands who claim to be eligible but were denied payments or access.

The other alleged nightmare is that it would lead to fiscal chaos. The result would be less government spending on business, education, jobs, and housing programs that directly benefit the poor and working-class Blacks. It would be a case of robbing Peter to pay Paul, leaving both Peter and Paul the poorer for it.

Reparations have been lambasted as unfeasible, impractical, garbled, confused, muddled, and ill-focused. Conservatives charge that Democrats latched on to the issue to pander to its biggest and most rock-solid political base, African Americans. It's nothing but another case of grabbing at political correctness and woke quasi-culture to appease Black voters.

During the 2020 presidential campaign, a slew of Democratic contenders stumbled over themselves to snatch at racial correctness. Reparations advocacy was supposedly the linchpin for this. There was Kamala Harris, for instance, saying reparations were an opportunity "to correct course." There was Beto O'Rourke writing that reparations were among the "necessary steps to repair the damage done."

There was another Democratic presidential candidate, Julian Castro, asserting that we are "never going to fully heal as a country . . . until we've addressed"—with reparations—"the tremendous wrong that was done with slavery." More than a few critics noted that while these were bold words about reparations, none of these Democrats were willing to go much further than momentary campaign stump rhetoric on the issue.

Trump and McConnell did not need to cite the litany of stock arguments against reparations. They simply cited the impracticality of it and the more compelling fallback retort that the decades of government action and redress of racial bias and disparities have done much to close the economic gap between Blacks and whites.

That in turn has been the engine that has enabled Blacks to smash through the racial barriers to opportunity.

Therefore, they have gotten their reparations and then some. If polls are to be believed, the majority of all Americans, and that includes many Blacks, agree.

3

A Tough Sell—Guilt Notwithstanding

On May 1, 2022, Tulsa County District Judge Caroline Wall did something that the handful of living survivors of the Tulsa Massacre of 1921 thought they'd never live to see. She ruled, in a packed courtroom, that the lawsuit for reparations for the survivors of the massacre could go forward. The Tulsa massacre was certainly aptly named.

From May 31 to June 1, 1921, a white mob engaged in a colossal orgy of murder, rape, burning, and looting of the thriving Black business and financial section of Tulsa, Oklahoma. It was as near a planned, orchestrated, racial pogrom as America would ever witness. When the smoke cleared hundreds were dead, and millions of dollars' worth of property were lost.

There have been countless articles, books, and stories recounting the horror of those days and telling the stories of the dwindling number of survivors. The state of Oklahoma apologized for the terror in 1997. One hundred years later, on June 1, 2021, Tulsa Mayor G.T. Bynum added his and the city's apology: "The victims—men, women, young children—deserved better from their city, and I am so sorry they didn't receive it."

However, as of 2023—a hundred plus years since the grotesque quasi-genocide assault—not a penny had been shelled out to the survivors as reparations. Judge Wall's decision held out that faint possibility. Her decision also reopened the bigger issue of reparations for slavery. This has been one of the most hotly debated, contentious issues since Conyers introduced the first reparations-related bill in Congress in 1989. There have been countless studies, reports, news articles, and debates, and a proposed House commission to study the feasibility of reparations.

During this same period, payments have been made to Japanese Americans, various American Indian groups, and other affected individuals and groups for past injustices. Yet not one penny has been allocated for reparations in any form to African Americans.

Why is that? The easy answer is that there have been so many proposals put forth on how reparations could be made, for what, and to whom, that the issue has become hopelessly entangled. There's truth to that. But that's too easy. As mentioned, reparations are a tough sell, but it has little to do with hard dollars.

It wasn't just the slew of GOP obstructionists, conservative bloggers, websites, right-wing think tanks, and unreconstructed bigots who vehemently and reflexively opposed any talk of reparations payments for slavery. There were a lot of Democrats who couldn't stomach the idea of such payments either, even those who professed to back a study of reparations feasibility. The 2020 presidential election was a prime example.

Every 2020 Democratic presidential candidate signed onto the House measure to establish a reparations feasibility commission. Before top Democrats signed on to the commission, the demand for reparations was mostly viewed as a fringe issue touted by a motley mix of

Black separatists, zealots, and crackpots that respected mainstream civil rights leaders shunned.

However, the Democrats' support for such a study was mostly political symbolism. Biden did not push the issue. He did not dare talk about the need for slavery reparations to rural, blue-collar, less-educated white voters in the run-up to the election. These were the voters who did much to put Trump in the Oval Office in 2016. Biden hoped to appeal to some of these voters with his moderate, centrist, plain-speaking style.

Biden and his pick for Vice President, Kamala Harris, had to stay as mum as possible on the issue. It cost no political capital and posed no political danger to simply support a commission study that could take years to complete, and then do little more than make recommendations. In most cases, recommendations could be watered down, ignored, or outright rejected. There was a good reason for the Democrats to tread with caution on the issue.

*****

Every poll that was taken before and during the 2020 presidential elections on reparations for slavery repeatedly showed that most whites, and a large segment of Latino and Asian voters, opposed it. The same polls showed that a considerable number of Blacks either outright opposed reparations or were uncertain about making this too much of an issue.

Reparations advocates grabbed at every argument in the book to try and dent the wall of public resistance. They offered assurances that Black millionaires, corporate presidents, superstar athletes, and entertainers wouldn't get a dime of reparations money. They emphasized that reparations would go to programs to aid the Black poor and that it wouldn't guilt-trip all whites.

The arguments still fell on deaf ears. The reparations movement couldn't shake the public perception that it was a movement exclusively of, by, and for Blacks. There was deep suspicion that it was still nothing but a cash grab by Blacks for Blacks, for the past horror of slavery that whites who opposed reparations repeatedly insisted was decades ago and something they had nothing to do with.

Democratic Senator Bernie Sanders for a time was a leading 2020 Democratic presidential contender. He typified the wariness that top Democrats had of taking an activist stance on reparations. He voiced concern that reparations could be a potential minefield for Democrats. At first, like Biden, he said he didn't back reparations. But then he pivoted and jumped on the feasibility study bandwagon. This was a tepid compromise and sounded like a face-saving ploy, banking on the issue fading into obscurity.

The GOP loaded up its arsenal of attacks on the Democrats in the dozen or so states they had targeted in the 2020 presidential elections as the states that would determine who sat in Congress after the elections. They would tar the Democrats as far-out loons who wanted to push all kinds of wild socialist-tinged ideas on health care, climate control, green energy, education, and so on. They almost certainly would have added reparations support to the supposed screwball list of measures that a Democrat would press on the nation if the Democrats had full control of Congress.

If Democrats stayed on record to make reparations a legitimate public policy talking point, how much of a political risk was there? This also meant avoiding at all costs the appearance that reparations were a frivolous issue that was both politically divisive and racially polarizing. It was a delicate tight rope to walk. But top Democrats managed it because they well knew that reparations were a tough sell.

4

Nothing New in the Reparations Battles

The scene seemed surreal. There was then-President Ronald Reagan seated at the desk in the Oval Office on August 9, 1988. He was surrounded by leading Japanese American political, business, and civil rights leaders. The occasion was Reagan's signing of the congressionally-passed Civil Liberties Act of 1988.

Reagan was emphatic about the historic wrong of internment and the U.S. government's obligation to atone for it: "Yet no payment can make up for those lost years. So, what is most important in this bill has less to do with property than with honor, for here we admit a wrong." Still, it took decades of legal action, political agitation, petitions, appeals, demonstrations, and protests by tens of thousands of individuals and organizations to make that moment a reality.

The law did two immediate things. It awarded those surviving Japanese Americans who were interned during World War II—in what were charitably branded as internment or relocation centers, but in reality, were concentration camps-American style—twenty thousand dollars in cash for their suffering and persecution. There were 120,000 interned, and stripped of their property. The estimate is that these brutal actions cost those interned tens of millions in property and income loss.

The second accomplishment of the Act was that it mandated a formal apology by President Reagan, which he did make. Democratic Congressman Norman Mineta had been an internee along with his family. He played a major role in the long-term battle for an apology and reparations from the government. Mineta was tactful in recounting what the moment meant to Japanese Americans: "The country made a mistake, and admitted it was wrong. It offered an apology and a redress payment. To me, the beauty and strength of this country is that it is able to admit wrong and issue redress."

In this instance, it did. However, even on the internment and reparations issue, it still took massive political and legal battles that dragged on for years to get Reagan and Congress to the point of redressing, as Mineta put it, a monumental historic wrong. The opponents of any redress turned a blind eye to the congressionally-mandated study commission on internment and reparations. Then they fought tooth and nail against its recommendations for compensation.

They ignored the testimony of maltreatment by hundreds of witnesses who testified before the commission. They denounced the commission's inescapable conclusion, that the internment was a product of "race prejudice, war hysteria, and a failure of political leadership," not a military necessity. Then there was also the predictable fallback argument that slavery reparations opponents toss out endlessly: World War II internment happened decades ago, forget about it, and move on. Mineta noted that many congresspersons spouted that line: "They said this happened over forty years ago. Why should we keep talking about it?"

*****

While the fight for reparations for Japanese Americans illegally and wrongly interned during the war is the best-known example of the U.S. government admitting its role in perpetuating a historic wrong, it is not the only one. And in each case, the pattern is the same. The aggrieved and victimized have to fight long, costly, and painful political and legal battles to get redress.

The battle that ranks up with the fight for Japanese American reparations, that is almost as well known and fought for decades longer, was the battle for compensation to American Indian tribal groups for the theft of land, mineral rights, and their forced assimilation. That was accompanied by the serial breaking of treaties that the government had signed with tribal leaders to protect their lands.

The breakthrough in this case came in 1946. The congressionally-authorized Indian Claims Commission, after extensive review, hearings, and protests, eventually shelled out over a billion dollars to dozens of tribal groups. The government, though, made no formal apology for its prime role in the near extermination of Native Americans.

An apology for that finally did come in 2009. However, it was hedged. It was tucked inside a defense spending bill, and it used the most bland, non-indicting words. It characterized the extermination effort as "many instances of violence, maltreatment, and neglect inflicted on Native Peoples by citizens of the United States."

American Indians weren't the only indigenous American group that suffered theft of land, farms, and businesses at the U.S. government's direction—as well as the attempt to wipe out indigenous culture. The U.S. seized Hawaii in its nineteenth-century Manifest Destiny bid for global territorial expansion, power, and domination. The then Kingdom of Hawaii was a prime target and victim.

In the 1890s the U. S. government overthrew the kingdom and confiscated the Hawaiians' land for plantations to cultivate and export sugar, pineapple, and fruit, and for ranching. Immediately following World War I, Hawaiian political and civil rights leaders first made the demand that the lands stolen should be returned to Native Hawaiians.

The government took a small step to acknowledge the claim by permitting a relatively small number of Hawaiians to lease land for ninety-nine years for one dollar. The catch was that the land leased was not the prime agricultural and developed land that was seized. That land was excluded from the lease arrangement. It took another near century after the seizures for the U.S. government to finally issue a pro forma apology, in 1993, for its treatment of Native Hawaiians.

*****

There has been only one instance in which the U.S. government came close to admitting a historic wrong done to African Americans. That was for the monstrous Tuskegee experiments. This story is fairly well known. For four decades, the U.S. Health Service used at least four hundred African American men as human guinea pigs for medical experiments. The men had syphilis. Health officials—nurses, doctors, and government administrators—signed off on the denial of medical treatment to these men. The men were simply told when they raised questions about the lack of treatment that they were part of an "experiment."

The predictable happened. The men died quickly or had slow, painfully agonizing deaths. Most of the men were long dead when the story about these genocidal experiments broke nationally in the early 1970s. That ignited a firestorm of protest. It took a class-action lawsuit, and massive media and public denunciations, before the government acted.

In 1974 the government paid ten million dollars to the few survivors and agreed to cover healthcare and burial expenses for the men's families. That was not the end of it. In 2023, the Centers for Disease Control and Prevention (CDC) reported that fifteen descendants of the Tuskegee experiment victims were still being treated through the program. There was no apology or acknowledgment of wrongdoing by the government for its monstrous act.

Finally, in 1997, then-President Clinton formally apologized to the "hundreds of men betrayed." Historian James H. Jones summed up the impact the horror had on Blacks: "No scientific experiment inflicted more damage on the collective psyche of black Americans than the Tuskegee Study."

*****

There are two glaring but consistent takeaways from the rare times that the U.S. government has admitted wrongdoing for its action. The first is that it has rarely ever admitted any culpability for injustices done in its name. The second is that in those very rare instances when it has admitted wrongdoing and agreed to an apology and reparations for its grotesque acts, it has taken decades and a relentless legal and public battle for it to take that action. Every step of the way there has been bitter opposition to taking those actions.

In 2023, the slavery reparations fight is still in its relative infancy, in terms of tapping a national audience and getting attention from Democratic legislators. However, even at this early stage of the battle, the opposition to and arguments against reparations is ferocious and unyielding. The reluctance of governments, officials, and a wide body of the public to admit public wrongs done in its and their names won't change with the fight for reparations.

5

Show Me the Money

The inevitable question asked whenever yet another city or state sets up a commission to study the feasibility of slavery reparations payments has been: "Has any money ever been ladled out by state or municipal governments for righting a historic racial wrong to Blacks?" The answer is "Yes."

Yet, like so much on the issue of reparations that "yes" is layered with qualifiers and caveats. First, as of mid-2023, only a handful of cities have allocated funds for slavery-related reparations. Evanston, Illinois was the first out the door in 2019 with what it named its Restorative Housing Reparations Program. It disbursed fifteen thousand dollars to compensate for housing discrimination.

The problem was with who got assistance. Housing discrimination both in law and public policy had been rigidly in force for decades. For generations, tens of thousands of Blacks were denied loans and redlined by banks and insurance companies, and real estate agents colluded to shunt prospective Black homebuyers to one area of the city. When the reparations-style program was approved, six hundred persons applied. Yet only fifteen received any money for this historic discrimination.

With much fanfare, the Amherst Massachusetts Town Council in June 2021 approved a two-million-dollar reparations program. The problem there was that there was no immediate payout of money. It set a ten-year time frame for payments. The program had to be approved by two-thirds of the council to authorize any spending from it.

In July 2020, the City Council in Asheville, North Carolina made news when it unanimously apologized for the city's role in propping up slavery. It vowed to pay reparations. Again, the same problem cropped up as in every other pronouncement by a city to pay reparations—there were no specifics.

The Ashville council instead said that the program would entail "investments in Black areas to close the gap on the economic racial disparities." That was open-ended, nebulous, and vague enough to mean anything or nothing. Asheville City Council member Sheneika Smith instantly saw the problem: "We need to bring a red pen to the table to actually circle expenditures and really show how they related to the stated goals."

*****

In March 2023, one major city did make big headlines with a spectacular announcement about reparations. San Francisco's Board of Supervisors declared that the city would pay reparations for the decades of racial discrimination and economic deprivation to the city's Blacks. The headlines screamed that the board would pay five million dollars to eligible Blacks.

The board didn't stop with just the five million sum. Other recommendations included the elimination of personal debt and tax burdens, guaranteed annual incomes of at least $97,000 for 250 years, and homes for Blacks in San Francisco for just $1 a family.

Many scoffed at, ridiculed, and assailed the proposal. Beyond the attacks, though, there was more than just the devil in the details. In fact, the news headlines were deliberately sensationalist and just as false. The supposed proposal was only part of the draft recommendations from a city-established reparations feasibility committee. There was no eminent pay-out of five million dollars.

There was also not an actual timetable for approval, let alone for implementation. There was no cost analysis done, or any plans for how the program would be sustained. These were recommendations and nothing more. The city could reject or ignore them down the line.

The biggest question mark, though, was over the word "eligible." Just who could be a recipient? And how would that be determined? There were no clear answers. There was much doubt and uncertainty about just how far, how fast, and how sincere city officials actually were willing to go in making these breathtaking proposals for reparations.

Tinisch Hollins, the vice-chair of the city's African American Reparations Advisory Committee, noted: "I don't need to impress upon you the fact that we are setting a national precedent here in San Francisco. What we are asking for and what we're demanding is a real commitment to what we need to move things forward."

Eric McDonnell, chair of the advisory committee, went further: "There's still a veiled perspective that, candidly, Black folks don't deserve this. The number itself, $5m, is low when you consider the harm." Ironically, the one glimmer of possibility that the city might act on its reparation's proposal came from an expected opponent. That was the GOP. John Dennis, chair of the San Francisco Republican party, called the proposal "ridiculous." But he then added that San Francisco was the one city "where it could possibly pass."

Opponents and backers of the city's reparations proposal, as in other cities that debated reparations, agreed that the issue with taking meaningful action was that reparations proposals were just that—proposals. But San Francisco made big, splashy news only because it was the first major city to put an actual, some would say fantastic, dollar figure on reparations.

*****

Before San Francisco captured the news headlines with its millions in reparations declaration, mayors in a dozen other cities pledged in June 2021 to establish a reparations study commission in their cities. The mayors gave their reparations effort the catchy name of Mayors Organized for Reparations and Equity.

However, in each case, the mayors were deliberately or gropingly fuzzy about just what the commission would do and when it would do it. They gave no details about how much the commission would cost to establish, who would pay for it, and who would serve on the commission.

The mayors were careful, though, to insist in the face of the inevitable criticism that the commission was solely tasked with studying the feasibility of reparations. Some worried that their announcement was little more than politically correct grandstanding and questioned their commitment to eventually shelling out payments. St. Louis Mayor Tishaura Jones was one critic: "Black Americans don't need another study that sits on a shelf. We need decisive action to address the racial wealth gap holding communities back across our country."

Former Los Angeles Mayor Eric Garcetti sought to reassure the skeptics: "Let me be clear: Cities will never have the funds to pay for reparations on our own. When we have the laboratories of cities show that there is much more to embrace than to fear, we know that we can inspire national action as well." This was a thoughtful and even bold hope. Yet, the mayor's announcement remained words that might or might not be eventually translated into action.

Another problem beyond the political symbolism of establishing a reparations study commission was that, as in Evanston, Illinois, who the money would be disbursed to when there was an actual payout was a question mark. The number of recipients was either minuscule or the funds were minimal, or both.

Stockton, California was a prime example of both problems. Like San Francisco, the city made national news in 2019 when it announced that it would experiment with a guaranteed income program. Under the program's auspices, a small group of low-income people would receive cash payments each month with no restrictions on how they could spend it.

The amount of money for the program was small, and only a handful of residents qualified to receive the funds. How small? Each recipient received five hundred dollars a month, tops. How many received the funds? Only one hundred and twenty-five qualified. The program was not limited solely to Blacks, but included other low-income persons and immigrants.

*****

While the cities garnered sensational headlines on their reparations study commissions, state officials in a handful of states claimed they were also studying the possibility of establishing statewide reparations commissions. California was the first to act. In 2020, it established a reparations task force. Three years later in 2023, it was still the only state with a state commission. The task force was charged with the by-now standard template for reparations—to study the feasibility of it. It took two years to issue its first report.

The task force painted a grim picture of a state that many viewed as one of the nation's most racially enlightened liberal states, yet which perpetuated decades of systemic racial and institutional discrimination. The task force frankly admitted that its main role was educating California residents about the state's role in maintaining the institution of slavery and the decades of racial inequities. In its initial report, the commission did not specifically call for reparations payment.

Instead, its recommendations called for removing racial bias and discriminatory practices in standardized testing; compensating people deprived of profits for their work; investing in and creating free healthcare programs; and apologizing for acts of political disenfranchisement. The task force promised an even more comprehensive report in mid-2023. The expectation was that it would only flesh out the charges of state institutional racism with specific remedies and that one of them would be the question of payment.

In May 2023, the nine-member panel finally did put specific figures on what Blacks in California are owed and would receive for the myriad practices of discrimination the state practiced through the decades. Here's their proposal:

- An estimated $13,619 for each year of residency, based on a 71-year life expectancy, for harm caused by health care disparities.

- An estimated $115, 260 or $2,352 for each year of residency in the state within the 49-year period between 1971 and 2020 to compensate for mass incarceration and over-policing of Black communities.

- An estimated $148,099—or $3,366 for each year between 1933 and 1977 spent as a California resident—to account for discriminatory housing policies.

Again, the problem is the same as with all of the other reparations proposal dollar figures: it is just a proposal. The legislature and governor would have to approve any reparations deal. There was no timetable given for approval if it was to be forthcoming.

The time lag and the lack of specifics once again underscored the problem with reparations. How, what, when, and to whom would reparations be made to? This was the question that roiled, stymied, and beguiled every debate on reparations since Conyers first introduced his bill for a reparations study commission in 1989. Three decades later, nothing had changed.

6

Just How Much Is Owed

Attorney Cornelius Jones almost certainly knew that his demand of the U.S. government would be quickly and summarily dismissed. But the intrepid pioneer civil rights lawyer went ahead anyway. In 1915, he filed an unprecedented lawsuit against the government for sixty-eight million dollars in indemnities.

The indemnity was for unpaid slave labor. Jones specifically zeroed in on the South's principal staple cash product, cotton. Jones calculated that the government owed former slaves the money for their labor in cotton production. Jones contended that the U.S. Treasury directly benefited from the tax dollars that it reaped from the sale of cotton.

The government appealed and an appellate court quickly tossed out the case. It ruled that the government could not be sued without its consent. There was no earthly way a rigid Jim Crow government and its courts in 1915 would ever give any consent to a suit against it for slavery reparations.

But Jones' audacious—for the times—demand for reparations payments was the first legal challenge of any consequence to the U.S. government for its role in financially benefitting from slavery. Beyond Jones' bold and brave effort, he did something else with his suit. He put an actual dollar figure on the value of slave labor. The case went down in legal lore as the 'Cotton Tax Case." It set a precedent.

*****

It was a precedent that was based on a well-established economic and financial fact. Cotton was big, big business for a nascent, young, and fast-growing mercantile, shipping, banking, and most importantly, industrializing America in the early to mid-nineteenth century. Cotton was by far the most exported American commodity during those years. By the mid-1830s, cotton shipments accounted for more than half the value of all exports from the United States.

In his meticulously researched book, *Empire of Cotton: A Global History*, on the massive financial boost to the country from slave labor-driven cotton production, Harvard University historian Sven Becker noted: "Slavery was just as present in the counting houses of Lower Manhattan, the spinning mills of New England, and the workshops of budding manufacturers in the Blackstone Valley in Massachusetts and Rhode Island as on the plantations in the Yazoo-Mississippi Delta. The slave economy of the Southern states had ripple effects throughout the entire economy, not just shaping but dominating it."

There was more, in fact, much more to the outsized role slavery and cotton production played in building America's wealth, as well as that of Britain's financial and industrial ascent. Northern bankers provided much of the financing to the Southern planters for cotton production. The loans and credit the banks extended to them enabled them to purchase land and acquire even greater numbers of slave laborers. Northern merchants, moreover, organized the shipment of cotton into global markets.

Northern manufacturers and industrialists also provided massive funding for purchasing tools, textiles, and other goods needed to fuel the plantation economy. Cotton production was so integral to U.S. industrial and financial growth that one commentator called the financing of it by Northern banks and manufacturers "second slavery."

*****

Several economists and researchers examined the financial debt owed from this unpaid labor, plus the ensuing decades of racial income disparity. They have put varied dollar figures on the financial benefit from slavery to the U.S. for more than a century and a half after the end of slavery. The figure they claim is owed is not in the billions, but trillions. They start by assessing the chronic economic gap between Blacks and whites. The gap according to numerous studies has held steady for decades. The net worth of the average white family is ten times greater than the average Black family.

In a 2015 study, University of Connecticut researcher Thomas Craemer placed the figure at slightly over fourteen trillion dollars. He arrived at this figure by calculating the hours slaves worked between 1776 and 1865. He then multiplied that by the average wage at the time. Since decades have passed with no payout, he added interest at three percent. The lowest figure is three to four trillion dollars allegedly outstanding.

In every case, the amount tabulated for the labor was challenged. The critics claim the figure is based on flawed data, inflated time averages per worker, and what is counted as slave labor versus non-slave labor. Yet, even the critics of the financial methodology used did not disagree that billions in financial wealth were produced by slave labor.

*****

Another contentious question on the alleged debt owed is that assuming that a figure of multi-billions or trillions was generated in profit from slavery, how much should be paid out to African Americans in whatever form? In 2020, the Census Bureau estimated there were ten million African American households. The racial gap between white and Black families was estimated at nearly a quarter million dollars. That added up to about ten trillion dollars. To make up the gap, the estimated forty million plus Blacks in the U.S. would be entitled to slightly more than a quarter million dollars.

That raises yet another problem. Who would be eligible to get such a sum? Reparations advocates answer that a vast genealogical probe would be made to determine whose ancestors were held as chattel slaves. That's possible to a limited extent.

Extensive records were kept of some slave auctions, announcements in newspapers with the listing of the names and dates sold of slaves, letters, and family genealogical research records that pinpointed family members sold into slavery. The most careful research to identify individuals sold and connect them to living relatives would require a vast research machinery.

South Carolina Democratic congressman Jim Clyburn saw a problem with identifying slave ancestry. In an interview in September 2020, Clyburn said that he feared reparations "would lead to contested debates about who would be eligible due to the sprawling family trees that have evolved in the generations since slavery was abolished."

To skirt this problem, the less divisive answer is to fund targeted programs to aid the Black poor. These proposals have included tax cuts; business, health care, education, and housing special funds; scholarship funds; or other collective investments.

The most hotly debated question outside of whether reparations should be paid at all is where the money would come from. Reparations advocates are nearly unanimous as they point their finger at the U.S. government.

One proposal is to fund in the standard way the government has paid for many other major funding projects, from wars to making up major budget shortfalls. That's through deficit spending. This would not require any increases in taxes. This approach almost certainly would be a non-starter. No GOP congressperson or senator, and almost certainly a majority of Democrats would support that. Millions of taxpayers would loudly protest about the use of their tax dollars for reparations.

Another proposal is to tap the Federal Reserve banks and have them provide funding the way they did to Wall Street during the Great Recession in 2009: namely through loans, credits, and incentives.

The finger is also pointed at banks, life insurance companies, and universities for the financial largesse they also received from slavery. They, too, say reparations advocates, have an obligation to pay. Some firms and colleges have admitted their complicity in profiteering from the slave trade and slave labor. They have made profuse public apologies. But there has been almost no cash forthcoming for any compensation. The exception was a handful of colleges that announced programs to provide tuition and scholarships for a small number of Blacks.

A leading reparations advocate, Nkechi Taifa, recognized the frustrating fight it has been to put a satisfactory proposal forward to government and private firms that benefited from the slave trade for reparations payments. She's pressed them to "come up with a settlement or negotiation." In almost all cases, there's been little result.

There's no doubt that slavery was an enormously lucrative business. It generated fabulous profits for the slave masters, bankers, insurance companies, shippers, manufacturers, and industrialists. It was a major engine for U.S. industrial and financial growth and global expansion. Even if a penny were never to be paid out in reparations, that would remain a tormenting and undeniable fact.

7

What Germany Can Teach Us About Reparations

The photo has been shown countless times through the years since that momentous day, September 10, 1952. More than a dozen men are shown sitting around a table in Luxembourg. They were there to ink an historic deal. The men were top officials from the West German government and the Israeli government.

The deal was that the West German government would pay tens of billions in reparations to the Israeli government, to a survivor claims group, and to individual survivors of Nazi Germany's genocidal slaughter of Jews. It was the first time in the history of war, suffering, death, and victimization that a government had ever paid compensation to the victims of its murderous actions.

Then Israeli Prime Minister David Ben-Gurion declared that the precedent set by the agreement obliged a country that "oppressed, plundered and despoiled" a people "has been obliged to return part of his spoils."

Seventy years later, in September 2022, to mark the anniversary of that historic agreement to pay for genocide, Germany invited representatives of the major Holocaust survivor claims organization and Holocaust survivors to a ceremony at Berlin's Jewish Museum. On that occasion, German officials made another announcement. They said that the government would add more to the reparations pot. It would now pay an added one billion plus dollars for home care and added compensation for the still-living Holocaust survivors. That amount brought the total that the German government had paid out since the 1952 Luxembourg agreement to nearly eighty billion dollars.

"The extermination of European Jews by the Nazis left a horrific chasm, not only in global Jewry but in global humanity," Gideon Taylor, the president of the New York-based Conference on Jewish Material Claims Against Germany, noted. He added, "These agreements laid the groundwork for compensation and restitution for those survivors who had lost everything and continue to serve as the foundation for the ongoing negotiations on behalf of the estimated 280,00 Holocaust survivors living around the world."

One spokesperson for the Holocaust survivors group made a telling point that the suffering that the Holocaust wreaked on the survivors and their families was not a thing of the past. Decades later, many still suffered deep physical and emotional trauma. There were yet other significant benefits to Germany's admission of guilt for the slaughter and its willingness to pay for it. The admission and payments made a profound sea change in the attitudes of Jews toward Germany.

In 2014, the Konrad Adenauer Foundation polled one thousand Israelis on their views of Germany. Almost seventy percent of the respondents had a good or excellent opinion of the country. Germany was now their favorite European nation. Goodwill, forgiveness, reconciliation, and just plain doing the ethical and moral thing, marked a turning point in German and Jewish relations.

*****

Another important aspect of the German reparations payments was that it squarely addressed the question that has repeatedly stirred confusion, anger, and division in the reparations debate over slavery. Many whites who oppose reparations can't understand why they should feel guilt, let alone be responsible for paying reparations for slavery with their tax dollars.

They argue that while slavery was an horrendous act, they had nothing to do with it since it happened decades, or a century or more, before they were born. Or they argue that their immigrant fore parents came to America decades after slavery was abolished. In 1985, the German government gave the best answer to that contentious question.

German president Richard von Weizsacker sharply noted, "The vast majority of today's population were either children then or had not been born. But their forefathers have left them a grave legacy. All of us, whether guilty or not, whether old or young, must accept the past. We are all affected by its consequences and liable for it."

Still, many slavery reparations critics don't buy this. They agree that the Germans did the right thing by paying and continuing to pay reparations to Holocaust survivors and the Israeli government. Yet in comparing slavery and the Holocaust, they are not the same thing. The Holocaust, they say, was relatively recent. There are still many actual survivors alive. The money was specifically earmarked to pay for specific financial, educational, and medical needs of those survivors.

Stuart E. Eizenstat, who served as a principal negotiator during the Carter, Clinton, and Obama administrations of Holocaust survivor claims, takes a nuanced view of the issue. He reiterated this difference, saying: "The common thread running through these U.S.-led negotiations and those of the Claims Conference is that restitution has come from the direct perpetrators of the crimes and has gone largely to those who directly suffered and survived, and, in some cases, their direct heirs."

At the same time, he made clear that there are still many things the U.S. government could do, from a formal apology for slavery to an array of special economic and legislative initiatives that would boost aid to education, business, health care, and job programs for Blacks. Impoverished Blacks, as with the Holocaust survivors, are the direct heirs of, if not slaves, then of slavery. This view also ignores the fact that many reparations advocates have not asked for direct cash payments but for the very same type of economic and legislative initiatives that he called for as a form of reparations for the historic wrongs.

*****

This well-intentioned view also soft-pedals the devastating impact that slavery has on every measurable social, health, business, educational, and economic disparity that has shackled and continues to shackle generations of African Americans. Those invisible chains still hideously distort American race relations.

Thomas Craemer, an associate professor of public policy at the University of Connecticut, says "Using distance and time as an argument" against reparations is damaging, "because it says if you commit a historical injustice and then you wait long enough, it doesn't count anymore."

There was some fear that Germany's agreement to pay reparations might stir public anger, resentment, and backlash. Polls showed at the time of the Luxembourg agreement that the great majority of Germans opposed the reparations payments. This was a false fear. There was no backlash. The watchwords for the payments instead became reconciliation and the restoration of moral dignity.

The Luxembourg agreements were not a slam dunk. It wasn't simply a case of German officials, let alone most Germans, falling on their knees, beating their chests, and asking for forgiveness and atonement. They had very mixed feelings about shelling out their tax dollars to the survivors and to the Israeli government.

Many were adamant that they were not responsible for Jewish suffering as individuals and therefore owed nothing. It took time for the government to get to the point of a payment agreement. But the payments, in the end, accomplished the most important result. They directly confronted a hideous period in the nation's past.

Lily Gardner Feldman, a fellow at Johns Hopkins University's American Institute for Contemporary German Studies, observed, "If you don't deal with the past, it's always going to be there." She saw a direct parallel between what Germany did and what the U.S. won't but should do on reparations for slavery's curse.

"The German process has been long, continuous, and difficult. One can expect that in the American case."

8

What John Conyers Asked for in His Reparations Bill

HR 3745 IH

101st CONGRESS

1st Session

 H. R. 3745

To acknowledge the fundamental injustice, cruelty, brutality, and inhumanity of slavery in the United States and the 13 American colonies between 1619 and 1865 and to establish a commission to examine the institution of slavery, subsequent de jure and de facto racial and economic discrimination against African Americans, and the impact of these forces on living African Americans, to make recommendations to the Congress on appropriate remedies, and for other purposes.

IN THE HOUSE OF REPRESENTATIVES

November 20, 1989

Mr. CONYERS introduced the following bill; which was referred to the Committee on the Judiciary

A BILL

To acknowledge the fundamental injustice, cruelty, brutality, and inhumanity of slavery in the United States and the 13 American colonies between 1619 and 1865 and to establish a commission to examine the institution of slavery, subsequent de jure and de facto racial and economic discrimination against African Americans, and the impact of these forces on living African Americans, to make recommendations to the Congress on appropriate remedies, and for other purposes.

Be it enacted by the Senate and House of Representatives of the United States of America in Congress assembled,

SECTION 1. SHORT TITLE.

This Act may be cited as the `Commission to Study Reparation Proposals for African Americans Act'.

SEC. 2. FINDINGS AND PURPOSES.

(a) FINDINGS- The Congress finds that--

(1) approximately 4,000,000 Africans and their descendants were enslaved in the United States and the colonies that became the United States from 1619 to 1865;

(2) the institution of slavery was constitutionally and statutorily sanctioned by the Government of the United States from 1789 through 1865;

(3) the slavery that flourished in the United States constituted an immoral and inhumane deprivation of Africans' life, liberty, African citizenship rights, and cultural heritage, and denied them the fruits of their own labor; and

(4) sufficient inquiry has not been made into the effects of the institution of slavery on living African Americans and society in the United States.

(b) PURPOSE- The purpose of this Act is to establish a commission to--

(1) examine the institution of slavery which existed from 1619 through 1865 within the United States and the colonies that became the United States, including the extent to which the Federal and State governments constitutionally and statutorily supported the institution of slavery;

(2) examine de jure and de facto discrimination against freed slaves and their descendants from the end of the Civil War to the present, including economic, political, and social discrimination;

(3) examine the lingering negative effects of the institution of slavery and the discrimination described in paragraph (2) on living African Americans and on society in the United States;

(4) recommend appropriate ways to educate the American public of the Commission's findings;

(5) recommend appropriate remedies in consideration of the Commission's findings on the matters described in paragraphs (1) and (2); and

(6) submit to the Congress the results of such examination, together with such recommendations.

SEC. 3. ESTABLISHMENT AND DUTIES.

(a) ESTABLISHMENT- There is established the Commission to Study Reparation

Proposals for African Americans (hereinafter in this Act referred to as the 'Commission').

(b) DUTIES- The Commission shall perform the following duties:

(1) Examine the institution of slavery which existed within the United States and the colonies that became the United States from 1619 through 1865. The Commission's examination shall include an examination of--

(A) the capture and procurement of Africans;

(B) the transport of Africans to the United States and the colonies that became the United States for the purpose of enslavement, including their treatment during transport;

(C) the sale and acquisition of Africans as chattel property in interstate and intrastate commerce; and

(D) the treatment of African slaves in the colonies and the United States, including the deprivation of their freedom, exploitation of their labor, and destruction of their culture, language, religion, and family.

(2) Examine the extent to which the Federal and State governments of the United States supported the institution of slavery in constitutional and statutory provisions, including the extent to which such governments prevented, opposed,

or restricted efforts of freed African slaves to repatriate to their home land.

(3) Examine Federal and State laws that discriminated against freed African slaves and their descendants during the period between the end of the civil war and the present.

(4) Examine other forms of discrimination in the public and private sectors against freed African slaves and their descendants during the period between the end of the civil war and the present.

(5) Examine the lingering negative effects of the institution of slavery and the matters described in paragraphs (1), (2), (3), and (4) on living African Americans and on society in the United States.

(6) Recommend appropriate ways to educate the American public of the Commission's findings.

(7) Recommend appropriate remedies in consideration of the Commission's findings on the matters described in paragraphs (1), (2), (3), and (4). In making such recommendations, the Commission shall address, among other issues, the following questions:

(A) Whether the Government of the United States should offer a formal apology on behalf of the people of the United States for the perpetration of gross human rights violations on African slaves and their descendants.

(B) Whether African Americans still suffer from the lingering affects of the matters described in paragraphs (1), (2), (3), and (4).

(C) Whether, in consideration of the Commission's findings, any form of compensation to the descendants of African slaves is warranted.

(D) If the Commission finds that such compensation is warranted, what should be the amount of compensation, what form of compensation should be awarded, and who should be eligible for such compensation.

(c) REPORT TO CONGRESS- The Commission shall submit a written report of its findings and recommendations to the Congress not later than the date which is one year after the date of the first meeting of the Commission held pursuant to section 4(c).

SEC. 4. MEMBERSHIP.

(a) NUMBER AND APPOINTMENT- (1) The Commission shall be composed of 7 members, who shall be appointed, within 90 days after the date of enactment of this Act, as follows:

(A) Three members shall be appointed by the President.

(B) Three members shall be appointed by the Speaker of the House of Representatives.

(C) One member shall be appointed by the President pro tempore of the Senate.

(2) All members of the Commission shall be persons who are especially qualified to serve on the Commission by virtue of their education, training, or experience, particularly in the field of African American studies.

(b) TERMS- The term of office for members shall be for the life of the Commission. A vacancy in the Commission shall not affect the powers of the Commission, and shall be filled in the same manner in which the original appointment was made.

 (c) FIRST MEETING- The President shall call the first meeting of the Commission within 120 days after the date of the enactment of this Act, or within 30 days after the date on which legislation is enacted making appropriations to carry out this Act, whichever date is later.

(d) QUORUM- Four members of the Commission shall constitute a quorum, but a lesser number may hold hearings.

(e) CHAIR AND VICE CHAIR- The Commission shall elect a Chair and Vice Chair from among its members. The term of office of each shall be for the life of the Commission.

(f) COMPENSATION- (1) Except as provided in paragraph (2), each member of the Commission shall receive compensation at the daily equivalent of the annual rate of basic pay payable for GS-18 of the General Schedule under section 5332 of title 5, United States Code, for each day, including travel time, during which he or she is engaged in the actual performance of duties vested in the Commission.

(2) A member of the Commission who is a full-time officer or employee of the United States or a Member of Congress shall receive no additional pay, allowances, or benefits by reason of his or her service on the Commission.

(3) All members of the Commission shall be reimbursed for travel, subsistence, and other necessary expenses incurred

by them in the performance of their duties to the extent authorized by chapter 57 of title 5, United States Code.

SEC. 5. POWERS OF THE COMMISSION.

(a) HEARINGS AND SESSIONS- The Commission may, for the purpose of carrying out the provisions of this Act, hold such hearings and sit and at such times and at such places in the United States, and request the attendance and testimony of such witnesses and the production of such books, records, correspondence, memoranda, papers, and documents, as the Commission considers appropriate. The Commission may request the Attorney General to invoke the aid of an appropriate United States district court to require, by subpoena or otherwise, such attendance, testimony, or production.

(b) POWERS OF SUBCOMMITTEES AND MEMBERS- Any subcommittee or member of the Commission may, if authorized by the Commission, take any action which the Commission is authorized to take by this section.

(c) OBTAINING OFFICIAL DATA- The Commission may acquire directly from the head of any department, agency, or instrumentality of the executive branch of the Government, available information which the Commission considers useful in the discharge of its duties. All departments, agencies, and instrumentalities of the executive branch of the Government shall cooperate with the Commission with respect to such information and shall furnish all information requested by the Commission to the extent permitted by law.

SEC. 6. ADMINISTRATIVE PROVISIONS.

(a) STAFF- The Commission may, without regard to section 5311(b) of title 5, United States Code, appoint and fix the compensation of such personnel as the Commission considers appropriate.

(b) APPLICABILITY OF CERTAIN CIVIL SERVICE LAWS- The staff of the Commission may be appointed without regard to the provisions of title 5, United States Code, governing appointments in the competitive service, and without regard to the provisions of chapter 51 and subchapter III of chapter 53 of such title relating to classification and General Schedule pay rates, except that the compensation of any employee of the Commission may not exceed a rate equal to the annual rate of basic pay payable for GS-18 of the General Schedule under section 5332 of title 5, United States Code.

(c) EXPERTS AND CONSULTANTS- The Commission may procure the services of experts and consultants in accordance with the provisions of section 3109(b) of title 5, United States Code, but at rates for individuals not to exceed the daily equivalent of the highest rate payable under section 5332 of such title.

(d) ADMINISTRATIVE SUPPORT SERVICES- The Commission may enter into agreements with the Administrator of General Services for procurement of financial and administrative services necessary for the discharge of the duties of the Commission. Payment for such services shall be made by reimbursement from funds of the Commission in such amounts as may be agreed upon by the Chairman of the Commission and the Administrator.

(e) CONTRACTS- The Commission may--

(1) procure supplies, services, and property by contract in accordance with applicable laws and regulations and to the extent or in such amounts as are provided in appropriations Acts; and

(2) enter into contracts with departments, agencies, and instrumentalities of the Federal Government, State agencies, and private firms, institutions, and agencies, for the conduct of research or surveys, the preparation of reports, and other activities necessary for the discharge of the duties of the Commission, to the extent or in such amounts as are provided in appropriation Acts.

SEC. 7. TERMINATION.

The Commission shall terminate 90 days after the date on which the Commission submits its report to the Congress under section 3(c).

SEC. 8. AUTHORIZATION OF APPROPRIATIONS.

To carry out the provisions of this Act, there are authorized to be appropriated $8,000,000.

Conclusion

A clearly chagrined White House Press Secretary Karine Jean-Pierre gave a short, snappy answer during a June 13, 2022, press briefing to the question of whether Biden would sign an Executive Order creating a White House reparations commission: "The president's position hasn't changed." That was her polite way of saying "No," that Biden wouldn't sign the Executive Order on reparations.

This was essentially the same answer that Jean-Pierre's predecessor as Biden's press secretary, Jen Psaki, gave when asked the same question a year earlier, in 2021: "We'll see what happens through the legislative process."

Biden was again pressed hard to sign the order simply because in the two years since the House Judiciary Committee established a reparations study commission in 2021, Congress had done nothing further on the issue. There was no sign that that would change in the foreseeable future. In May 2022, a dozen civil rights and religious groups sent a letter to Biden demanding he sign an executive order to study reparations. That didn't move him to act, either.

Biden at no point gave any hint that he'd take unilateral action by signing an Executive Order putting the White House's official stamp on a reparations study, let alone actual payments. During the presidential campaign, he minced no words when asked about reparations for Blacks. In an address to an audience in Spartanburg, South Carolina in February 2020, he was emphatic on the issue: "I support that study (of reparations)—let's see where that takes us."

Five months later, in July, with much fanfare, he issued a sweeping "racial equity" plan for combatting institutional racism in America. There was not one word about reparations, a reparations study commission, or any hint of support from him for either. The omission raised eyebrows and left many Blacks who ardently back reparations wondering which Biden to believe on reparations.

*****

Biden was not being insensitive, evasive, or non-committal on reparations because he thought it was a bad idea. He sat squarely on the hot seat on reparations because the issue has always been thorny, demanding, and contentious. Former President Obama, for instance, who early on flatly opposed the idea, eventually came around and called it an issue that merited a look. But that was a far cry from saying unequivocally that he backed reparations payments. However, with so many Democratic political heavy hitters seemingly on board on the issue, the implication was that there would soon be some action on some form of payment.

There have been a range of plans offered that entail some form of reparations be it tax credits or more funding for education, child care, and health care for Blacks. But if Democrats really embraced the idea, then the next question has always been: how hard would they be willing to push the issue as a major policy issue?

Democratic officials all inevitably looked hard over their shoulders before answering that question. They looked at the polls that have been taken on slavery reparations that consistently show that most whites oppose it. The GOP, along with a parade of conservative writers, analysts, and think tanks have staunchly opposed reparations.

Top Democrats looked hard at the time involved to take on the issue, the staggering expenses, and questions about where the money would come from and how it would be dispersed. They looked hard at the question of just who would get whatever payments were ultimately paid out. Most importantly, they looked hard at the potential political downside for winning elections if there was too vigorous a push for reparations.

The reparations movement would never possess the inherent racial egalitarianism of the civil rights movement. If the focus was solely to compensate the descendants of Black slaves and whipsaw whites for modern-day racism, the possibility of getting any traction, as shown, would be near impossible.

*****

Yet, there is a larger question that has remained. That is the ethical, the moral need to right an historical wrong. Whether it's called reparations or not, there is an outstanding debt that is owed for the catastrophic suffering of slavery and its hideous legacy that still entraps millions of Blacks more than a century and a half after the formal abolition of slavery.

The government could repay part of the debt owed while correcting at least some of the racial inequity and imbalances by pumping more funds into specific projects, such as AIDS/HIV education and prevention, remedial education, job skills and training, drug and alcohol counseling and rehabilitation, computer access, and literacy training. Such projects would boost the Black poor, not gut public revenues, and, most importantly, not finger all whites as culpable for slavery.

The issue certainly will not go away. By 2023, nearly every civil rights and social justice organization had endorsed reparations payments to Blacks in one form or another. The United Nations issued a report in 2016 calling not only for reparations for slavery but also for police killings. Nearly every Caribbean nation had established a commission to demand reparations from former European slave trading countries.

A raft of universities, corporations, and banks have done public *mea culpa* for their enrichment from slavery. More than a dozen big city mayors and city councils, as of mid-2023, had pledged to set up their own city's reparations study commission. More cities almost certainly over time will do the same.

The prime architect of the modern-day call for reparations, John Conyers, penned a letter in 2017 to congressional representatives. He urged action on his call for a reparations study commission. He was precise: "the harm caused by slavery has reverberated for centuries and impacted descendants. After decades of Jim Crow segregation, there's been racial discrimination and policies that still affect many African Americans today in education, housing, healthcare, and criminal justice."

Randall Robinson, the author of the groundbreaking book The Debt: What America Owes to Blacks, was even more emphatic and prophetic: "If African Americans will not be compensated for the massive wrongs and social injuries inflicted upon them by their government during and after slavery then there is no chance that America can solve its racial problems."

Conyers, in his softer, more analytic way, Robinson in his blunt and brutal way, and reparations opponents and advocates in their polar opposite ways, are all saying this: the question of reparations will not go away, and as long as it doesn't, it will remain yet another of America's tortured, racially divisive issues.

Sources

"H.R.3745 - Commission to Study Reparation Proposals for African Americans Act," U.S. Congress, October 24, 1990, https://www.congress.gov/bill/101st-congress/house-bill/3745/text.

Rashawn Ray and Andre Perry, "Why We Need Reparations for Black Americans," *Policy 2020 Brookings*, April 15, 2020, https://www.brookings.edu/policy2020/bigideas/why-we-need-reparations-for-black-americans/.

Fabiola Cineas, "Reviving the Case for Reparations," *Vox*, September 1, 2022, https://www.vox.com/podcasts/2022/9/1/23330727/reparations-case-nkechi-taifa.

Donna M. Owens, "Veteran Congressman Still Pushing for Reparations in a Divided America," *NBC*, February 19, 2017, https://www.nbcnews.com/news/nbcblk/rep-john-conyers-still-pushing-reparations-divided-america-n723151.

Jacquelyne Germain, "Reparations for Black Americans: Here's What Some State and Local Governments are Doing," *CNN*, July 13, 2022, https://www.cnn.com/2022/07/13/us/reparations-state-local-commission-reaj/index.html.

William Cummings, "Trump Says Reparations Debate is 'Interesting' But Doesn't 'see it happening," *USA*

Today, June 25, 2019, https://www.usatoday.com/
story/news/politics/onpolitics/2019/06/25/trump-
slave-descendants-reparations/1557041001/.

Kevin Freking, "Biden Backs Studying Reparations
as Congress Considers Bill." *AP News*,
February 17, 2021, https://apnews.com/
article/biden-study-reparations-congress-
e3c045ece4d0e0eae393a18a09a4a37e.

Richard A. Epstein, "The Case Against Reparations
for Slavery," *Hoover Institution*, May 27, 2014,
https://www.hoover.org/research/case-against-
reparations-slavery.

Jennifer Luden, "Cities may be debating reparations,
but here's why most Americans oppose the
idea," *NPR*, March 27, 2023, https://www.npr.
org/2023/03/27/1164869576/cities-reparations-
white-black-slavery-oppose.

Graham Hillard, "The Other Case Against Reparations,"
National Review, July 22, 2019, https://www.
nationalreview.com/2019/07/the-other-case-
against-reparations/.

Sean Neumann, "Tulsa's Mayor Apologizes for City's
'Failure to Protect' Black Community in 1921 Race
Massacre," *People*, June 1, 2021, https://people.
com/politics/tulsa-mayor-apologizes-for-citys-
role-in-1921-tulsa-race-massacre/.

Dale Nelson, "Payment to Interned Japanese-
Americans get Reagan's OK," *AP News*,

August 10, 1988, https://apnews.com/
article/312dbf84b9b11b603696b8fb0c53c960.

Erin Blakemore, "The Thorny History of Reparations
in the United States," *History*. August 29, 2019,
https://www.history.com/news/reparations-
slavery-native-americans-japanese-internment.

Dylan Matthews, "Six times victims have received
reparations-including four in the US," *Vox*, May 23,
2014, https://www.vox.com/2014/5/23/5741352/
six-times-victims-have-received-reparations-
including-four-in-the-us.

Adeel Hassan, "America Has Tried Reparations Before,
Here Is How It Went," *NY Times*, June 6, 2019,
https://www.nytimes.com/2019/06/19/us/
reparations-slavery.html.

AP, "Amherst Creates Fund to Pay Reparations to Black
Residents," *NBC*, June 25, 2021, https://www.
nbcnews.com/news/nbcblk/amherst-creates-fund-
pay-reparations-black-residents-rcna1273.

Lois Beckett, "San Francisco backs reparations plans,
including $5m to eligible Black adults," *The
Guardian*, March 14, 2023, https://www.
theguardian.com/us-news/2023/mar/14/san-
francisco-reparation-plans-black-residents.

AP, "11 US Mayors Commit to Developing Pilot Projects
for Reparations," *NPR*, June 18, 2021, https://
www.npr.org/2021/06/18/1008242159/11-u-s-
mayors-commit-to-developing-pilot-projects-for-
reparations.

Adam Beam, "11 Mayors Commit to Reparations Pilot
        Projects," *LA Times*, June 18, 2021, https://www.
        latimes.com/world-nation/story/2021-06-18/
        mayors-commit-to-develop-reparations-
        pilot-projects.

Jeanne Kaung, "Stockton Guaranteed Income Program
        Limits," *KQED*, April 12, 2019, https://www.
        kqed.org/news/11946467/study-shows-limits-
        of-stocktons-guaranteed-income-program-
        during-pandemic.

Sven Beckert, "America's first big business? Not the
        railroads, but slavery," *PBS*, February 12, 2015,
        https://www.pbs.org/newshour/nation/americas-
        first-big-business-railroads-slavery.

Dina Gerdeman, "The Clear Connection between
        Slavery and American Capitalism," *Forbes*,
        May 3, 2017, https://www.forbes.com/sites/
        hbsworkingknowledge/2017/05/03/the-clear-
        connection-between-slavery-and-american-
        capitalism/?sh=4e39bee17bd3.

Jacob Jarvis, "After Reparations Study Suggests $151
        Million for Each African American, Experts Say
        Money Alone Isn't Enough," *Newsweek*, July 17,
        2020, https://www.newsweek.com/reparations-
        slavery-cost-more-just-money-1518649.

Samara Lynn, "What America owes: How reparations
        would look and who would pay," *ABC News*,
        September 27, 2020, https://abcnews.go.com/
        Business/america-owes-reparations-pay/
        story?id=72863094.

Fabiola Cineas, "Reviving the Case for Reparations,"
    Vox, September 1, 2022, https://www.vox.com/
    podcasts/2022/9/1/23330727/reparations-case-
    nkechi-taifa.

Ta-Nehisi Coates, "Slavery Made America." *The Atlantic*,
    June 24, 2014. https://www.theatlantic.com/
    business/archive/2014/06/slavery-made-
    america/373288/

AP, "Germany marks 70 years of compensating Holocaust
    survivors with payment for home care," *ABC News*,
    September 15, 2022, https://www.nbcnews.com/
    news/world/nazi-germany-holocaust-survivors-
    compensation-payment-home-care-rcna47862.

Annabelle Timsit, "The blueprint the US can follow to
    finally pay reparations," *Quartz*, October 13,
    2020, https://qz.com/1915185/how-germany-paid-
    reparations-for-the-holocaust.

Stuart E. Eizenstat, "What Holocaust Restitution Taught
    Me About Slavery Reparations," *Politico*, October
    27, 2019, https://www.politico.com/magazine/
    story/2019/10/27/slavery-reparations-holocaust-
    restitution-negotiations-229881/.

Lois Beckett, "San Francisco backs reparations plans,
    including $5m to Eligible Black adults," *The
    Guardian*, March 14, 2023, https://www.
    theguardian.com/us-news/2023/mar/14/san-
    francisco-reparation-plans-black-residents.

IBW21, "My Reparations Bill-HR 40," *IBW.org*, October 3, 2013, https://ibw21.org/commentary/my-reparations-bill-hr-40/.

Gerren Keith Gaynor, "Black advocates challenge Biden on reluctance to sign executive order for reparations commission," *Yahoo! News*, June 22, 2022, https://news.yahoo.com/black-advocates-challenge-biden-reluctance-143000320.html?fr=sycsrp_catchall.

Beatrice Peterson, "Advocates call on Biden to act on reparations study by Juneteenth," *ABC News*, June 17, 2022, https://abcnews.go.com/Politics/advocates-call-biden-act-reparations-study-juneteenth/story?id=85418510.

Donna M. Owens, "Veteran Congressman Still Pushing for Reparations in a Divided America," *NBC*, February 19, 2017, https://www.nbcnews.com/news/nbcblk/rep-john-conyers-still-pushing-reparations-divided-america-n723151.

Centers for Disease Control and Prevention, "The Syphilis Study at Tuskegee Timeline," https://www.cdc.gov/tuskegee/timeline.htm.

Bibliography

Araujo, Ana Lucia. *Reparations for Slavery, and the Slave Trade: A Transnational and Comparative History.* New York: Bloomsbury Academic, 2017.

Baradaran, Mehrsa. *The Color of Money: Black Banks and the Racial Wealth Gap.* Cambridge, MA: Belknap Press: An Imprint of Harvard University Press, 2019.

Becker, Sven. *Empire of Cotton: A Global History.* New York: Vintage, 2015.

Brown, Gene. *Reparations for Slavery and Disenfranchisement to African Americans: Four Hundred Years.* S.l.: Xlibris, 2007.

Coates, Ta-Nehisi. *Study Guide: The Case for Reparations by Ta-Nehisi Coates.* S.l.: SuperSummary, 2020.

Cosby, Kevin W. *Getting to the Promised Land: Black America and the Unfinished Work of the Civil Rights Movement.* Louisville, KY: Westminster John Knox Press, 2021.

Darity, William. *The Black Reparations Project: A Handbook for Racial Justice.* Berkeley, CA: University of California Press, 2023.

Darity, William and Kristen Muller. *From Here to Equality: Reparations for Black Americans in the Twenty-First Century.* Chapel Hill, NC: University of North Carolina Press, 2020.

Holland, Paula. *Reverse the Slavery Curse: Breaking the Black Magic Spells.* New York: Dunamis Media Group, 2022.

Howard, Kamm. *Laying the Foundation for Local Reparations: A Guide for Providing National Symmetry for Local Reparation Efforts.* Independently Published, 2020.

The Presidential Committee on the Legacy of Slavery. *The Legacy of Slavery at Harvard: Report and Recommendations of the Presidential Committee.* Cambridge, MA: Harvard University, 2022.

Robinson, Randall. *The Debt: What America Owes to Blacks.* New York: Dutton, 2000.

Rothstein, Richard. *The Color of Law: A Forgotten History of How Our Government Segregated America.* New York: Norton, 2018.

Taifa, Nkechi, *Reparations on Fire: How and Why It's Spreading Across America.* Washington, DC: House of Songhay II, 2022.

Taiwo, Olufhemi O., *Reconsidering Reparations (Philosophy of Race).* New York: Oxford University Press, 2022.

Various Authors. *Through the Eyes of a Slave: Written Accounts of American Slavery.* Los Angeles: Read & Co., 2020.

Wimbush, Raymond A. *Should America Pay? Slavery and the Raging Debate on Reparations.* New York: Amistad, 2003.

About the Author

Earl Ofari Hutchinson is the author of multiple books on race and politics in America. He is a political analyst and has appeared on MSNBC and on CNN. His books include the trilogy on the Obama Years: *The Obama Legacy; How Obama Governed: The Year of Crisis and Challenge*; and *How Obama Won*. His most recent books are *The Trump Challenge to Black America; From King to Obama: Witness to a Turbulent History*; and *Bring Back the Poll Tax— The GOP War on Voting Rights*.

Index